Bible Study

7 SESSIONS FOR SMALL GROUP
AND PERSONAL USE

Violence Against Women

Discovering El Roi,
The God Who Sees

Copyright ©Waverley Abbey Trust, 2023.

Published 2023 by Waverley Abbey Trust, a trading name of CWR, Waverley Abbey House, Waverley Lane, Farnham, Surrey GU9 8EP, UK. Registered Charity No. 294387. Registered limited company No. 1990308.

The right of Claudine Roberts to be identified as the author of this work has been asserted by her in accordance with the Copyright, Designs and Patents Act 1988, sections 77 and 78.

All rights reserved. No part of this publication may be reproduced, stored in a retrieval system, or transmitted, in any form or by any means, electronic, mechanical, photocopying, recording or otherwise, without the prior permission in writing of Waverley Abbey Resources.

For a list of National Distributors, visit waverleyabbeytrust.org/distributors

Unless otherwise indicated, all Scripture references are from the NIV, New International Version® Anglicised, NIV® Copyright © 1979, 1984, 2011 by Biblica, Inc.® Used by permission. All rights reserved worldwide.

Other Bible translations:

The Amplified Bible (AMP) Copyright © 2015 by The Lockman Foundation, La Habra, CA 90631. All rights reserved.

The Holy Bible, English Standard Version (ESV) is adapted from the Revised Standard Version of the Bible, copyright Division of Christian Education of the National Council of the Churches of Christ in the U.S.A. All rights reserved.

KJV – public domain.

Holy Bible, New Living Translation, copyright © 1996, 2004, 2015 by Tyndale House Foundation. Used by permission of Tyndale House Publishers, Inc., Carol Stream, Illinois 60188. All rights reserved.

THE MESSAGE, copyright © 1993, 2002, 2018 by Eugene H. Peterson. Used by permission of NavPress. All rights reserved. Represented by Tyndale House Publishers, Inc.

Every effort has been made to ensure that this book contains the correct permissions and references, but if anything has been inadvertently overlooked, the Publisher will be pleased to make the necessary arrangements at the first opportunity. Please contact the Publisher directly.

Concept development and editing by Waverley Abbey Trust.

Design and typesetting by Richard Lyall Design.

Printed and bound in the UK.

Paperback ISBN: 978-1-78951-445-2

eBook ISBN: 978-1-78951-486-5

Contents

4 INTRODUCTION TO THE COVER TO COVER SERIES

6 ABOUT THE AUTHOR

7 INTRODUCTION

11 WEEK 1
The God Who Sees Me (Hagar)

17 WEEK 2
God the Rescuer (Dinah)

23 WEEK 3
God the Father (Jephthah's Daughter)

29 WEEK 4
God the Loving Husband (The Unnamed Concubine)

35 WEEK 5
God the King of Kings (Tamar)

41 WEEK 6
God the Just Judge (The Woman Caught in Adultery)

47 WEEK 7
What Needs to Change?

53 LEADER'S NOTES

77 DAILY GUIDE

81 SIGNPOSTING

About Cover to Cover

The *Cover to Cover* Bible Study Guides are a popular series helping individuals and groups to engage with the Bible and to dig deeper.

The first studies were produced in 2002 by Selwyn Hughes and now cover more than 80 different themes, characters and books of the Bible, and compiled by various writers and Bible teachers.

How to get the best from the studies

The *Cover to Cover* studies are designed to be either worked through individually or in a group. Whichever way you are using the study we encourage you to begin with prayer, asking God through His Holy Spirit to work in your life through these studies. Then trust that He will!

Do allow enough time for the questions and exercises, not rushing through but allocating time to focus on questions that raise specific challenges.

If you are studying as a group you may find our online resources useful. Here you will find some extra video content and copies of the daily guide to distribute to the members. Visit **wvly.org/c2ccv** to discover what is available.

In group discussions do make use of the leader's notes at the end of the study. Ensure that you give everyone in the group time to share and avoid allowing one person to dominate conversation.

Please feel free to adapt the material according to your group's needs. Trust that God is with you, leading you and helping each one of you draw closer to Him.

About the Author

Written by Claudine Roberts

Claudine Roberts is a former human rights solicitor now working in communications for an international family of churches and preaching in her local church. She is married to Paul and they have three children. Like far too many women across the globe, Claudine has her own story of surviving sexual violence. She longs to see relationships between men and women transformed by the power of the gospel.

Introduction

The problem of male violence against women and girls has been around for generations. In fact, there are several detailed accounts of such violence in the Bible, beginning in Genesis. When was the last time you studied those stories or heard a church leader teaching on them?

The silence of the Church on this issue is a problem because it helps to perpetuate the violence. We are called to expose the works of darkness and bring them into the light. As followers of Jesus, we should be speaking out against injustice and oppression, including domestic abuse, sexual violence, child marriage, infanticide and other forms of violence against women and girls.

The World Health Organisation estimates that one third of all women worldwide will experience physical and/or sexual violence by a partner, or sexual violence by a non-partner.[1] This means gender-based violence very probably affects some of the women in your church and possibly in your small group. If we never talk about this injustice those women might feel like the topic is off limits and, as a result, they may feel unable to tell their own stories – stories of past suffering or stories of present danger. There are women in our churches who need to experience God's love for them through the healing of past hurts or through practical help to escape abuse. We want our churches to be safe places, where survivors and reporters of abuse are listened to, believed and loved.

1   WHO clinical and policy guidelines, *Responding to intimate partner violence and sexual violence against women*, 2013.

In the past, some of the biblical stories of violence against women and girls have been poorly interpreted, leading to victim-blaming and a culture of misogyny even within the Church. Our understanding of these Old Testament stories hasn't always matched up with our understanding of the character of God.

In the book of Exodus, we read that Moses asks God about His character, who He really is; what He's like. The very first thing God talks about is His compassion, or mercy. It's at the top of the list. God is concerned about our suffering. The Bible also tells us that God is love, He is the same yesterday, today and forever, and the kingdom of God is a kingdom of justice. More than that, God repeatedly speaks out specifically against violence. Then, in the pages of the New Testament, in Jesus we see a God who treats women with love, respect and dignity.

If we read the biblical stories of violence against women and girls in light of what we already know to be true about God's character, as revealed in the Word of God and in the person of Jesus, we find a God who cares deeply about women and about the relationship between the sexes. We find a God who sees each one of His children and is moved by their suffering. A God who had a plan all along to put things right, to bring an end to injustice; to end all violence.

The Leader's Notes at the end of this study guide will help you interpret these difficult passages of Scripture. They will guide you to see each story through the eyes of their female characters. They will also show you how each story points to Jesus, by examining how the actions of the male characters like Abraham, Jacob and David, often referred to as Bible 'heroes', fall short. Each story points to the need for a saviour, the Saviour.

The Daily Guide is designed to be used as part of your daily prayer time, to help you engage with this study in a deeper

INTRODUCTION

way. Before you start, think about when and how you might use the daily reflections, meditations and suggestions best in your own routine.

Some of the stories covered in this study are horrifically violent and difficult to read. Please be aware of your emotions as you read them and take a break whenever you need to. If you become aware of unresolved trauma in your own life, I would urge you to seek professional help from a trauma therapist in order to process it. You can find the contact details for helplines and organisations that offer support in the Signposting section at the back of this book. If you are in immediate danger please call the police on 999, or to report a crime please call 101 (in the UK).

My prayer is that this study guide will deepen your understanding of the biblical stories of violence against women and girls and increase your knowledge of the God of compassion who is moved by our suffering. I also pray that it will have a positive impact on all your relationships and help make your church a safe place for survivors of abuse.

WEEK ONE
The God Who Sees Me (Hagar)

Opening Exercise

Which of the names of God feels most significant for you right now? Briefly share why that is, if you are comfortable doing so. Is your choice related to something that has happened, or is happening, in your life?

Bible Readings

- Genesis 16
- Job 39:5–8
- Genesis 21:1–21

Optional Readings
- Genesis 17:1–13
- Genesis 12:10–20

Opening Our Eyes

In Genesis 16 Abraham and his wife Sarah[2] use their servant Hagar as a surrogate, to produce an heir, and in Genesis 21 Hagar and the child are banished from their home because of Sarah's jealousy. The story focuses on Abraham and God's promise to make him the father of many generations, so the message of Hagar's story can be easily missed or misinterpreted.

We aren't given much of Hagar's backstory, but we are told that she is Egyptian. Given that Abraham and Sarah spent time in Egypt earlier in their story (see Gen. 12), it is not unreasonable to deduce that Hagar entered Sarah's service while they were there. In fact, Genesis 12:16 even says Abraham acquired 'sheep and cattle, male and female donkeys, male and female servants, and camels' in Egypt. So we know where Hagar came from and we know her status as a servant in Abraham and Sarah's house, but that is all, until suddenly Hagar is introduced as the answer to Sarah's devastating infertility.

The violence and abuse of the first few verses of Genesis 16 is easy to minimise or miss entirely. Abraham and Sarah plan the rape of Hagar. You might wonder if this really is a story of rape. We will look at some other stories of rape in the Bible where that word is actually used (the rape of Dinah in Genesis 34 and the rape of Tamar in 2 Samuel 13), but it doesn't explicitly say here that Hagar doesn't consent. Some theologians do write about this story as if Hagar commits sexual sin too. It could be that the word for rape used in the stories of Dinah and Tamar in the original Hebrew (*chazaq*) isn't used here because that word denotes serious physical force. Those women were beaten up and raped. It could be that this was non-consensual sex with coercive control rather than physical force. Perhaps Hagar

---

2   Abram and Sarai are renamed Abraham and Sarah by God in Genesis 17, but to avoid confusion I will refer to them by those names throughout.

quietly complied with a sense of resignation and there were no kicks or punches. That's still rape.

Whether Hagar consented to sex with Abraham or not is important because it goes to the issue of whether Hagar sinned by sleeping with Abraham, or whether the sin was his and Sarah's alone. Whether Hagar sinned or not may not be wholly important to the biblical narrative, which centres around Abraham and Sarah, but in Hagar's story it is of great importance. To a survivor of rape, the issues of consent and blame really matter. It is all too easy for survivors of rape to blame themselves and take on the shame of that perceived sin. If we assume that Hagar consented to sex with Abraham and take the view that her behaviour was sinful, then we ignore the mismatch of power in their relationship and we leave it open for other oppressed and coerced women to assume guilt for their own abuse. It is also important for us to understand just how far Abraham and Sarah fell because of their lack of faith that God would fulfil His promise to them.

Notes

Discussion Starters

1. Do you think Hagar may have consented to bear a child for Abraham and Sarah, or is this really a story of rape?

2. Can you see two ways in which Abraham's actions were sinful? Are you surprised by how quickly Abraham's lack of faith led to serious sin?

3. Was Hagar the only person in the story who suffered trauma?

4. Who was the 'angel of the Lord' who found Hagar in the desert and why do you think he told Hagar to return to the house of Abraham and Sarah? Does this seem strange to you, in light of what you know about the character of God?

THE GOD WHO SEES ME (HAGAR)

5. Are you troubled by the angel of the Lord's prophecy about Ishmael? Why do you think Hagar didn't take his words as an insult?

6. Hagar called God El Roi, 'the One Who Sees Me'. What might this reveal about how Hagar felt?

7. Why didn't God just fulfil His promises to Abraham through Ishmael, instead of giving Abraham and Sarah a biological son?

8. Why did Abraham send Hagar and Ishmael away in Genesis 21? What does this tell us about Abraham's faith in God?

Personal Application

Abraham was a man of great faith, but even godly men are not immune to failure. Abraham's lack of faith in God led directly to his sexual abuse of Hagar. One mistake led to another and his sin had serious consequences for those around him. God wants us to take this as a warning. We are supposed to see how easy it is for us to fall into sin and that our sin has serious consequences.

For Hagar, the result of Abraham and Sarah's sin was that she believed she didn't matter, to God or to anyone. Are you believing a lie as the result of someone else's sin against you? God saw Hagar and showed her that she mattered. God sees you too; take a moment to reflect on the truth that you matter to Him.

Seeing Jesus in the Scriptures

In reading Hagar's story, we are supposed to grasp that Abraham and Sarah's actions were sinful – against Hagar and against God. Rape is abhorrent to God and we are supposed to be outraged by it. God met Hagar in the wilderness, invited her into relationship with Him and made promises to her for the future, because she was precious to Him. God invites us into relationship with Himself today, through His Son Jesus.

Abraham was the leader of God's family, the most righteous man around, but even he fell short. He lacked faith in God and failed to protect his people from sin and the consequences of sin. The family of God needed a saviour; the Saviour. Hagar's story points to the need for Jesus. He meets each of us where we are and invites us into relationship with Him, just as God met Hagar in the desert.

WEEK TWO
God the Rescuer (Dinah)

Opening Exercise

What is your favourite fairy tale? Is it a story of good and evil? Of someone being rescued from peril? Explain why it is your favourite to those in the room, if you are happy to.

Bible Readings

- Genesis 34

Optional Readings
- Deuteronomy 22:28–29
- Genesis 49:5–7
- Genesis 17:11
- Genesis 46:10

Opening Our Eyes

In Genesis 34 Jacob's daughter Dinah is kidnapped and raped by Shechem, a Canaanite. The story focuses on the consequences of the rape rather than the crime itself.

If you're anything like me, you might approach a story like this with the expectation that there will be 'goodies and baddies' in the story. Growing up on fairy tales and Disney films has done me a disservice, particularly when it comes to reading the Bible. Children's work in churches can often reinforce the idea of Bible 'heroes'. Spoiler alert! There isn't a hero in Dinah's story.

It is generally agreed that Dinah was very young when Shechem raped her, although she was probably of marriageable age in that culture. This isn't a major factor in the story, but it does us good to read the Bible with an awareness of the culture of the day and of our own. Dinah's young age adds to our modern-day outrage at the crime, because we feel even more convinced that she should have been protected.

We read that 'Dinah… went out to visit the women of the land' (Gen. 34:1). In the past, some have interpreted this as foolish and risky, which has led to victim-blaming. There are things women do to keep themselves safe from violent men, like walking with our keys grasped between our fingers in case we need to use them as a weapon, walking past our front door if someone has been walking behind us for a while, or crossing the street when we see men who look like they might be drunk.[3] Do you think about your safety daily like this? Have you ever considered that some people have to think about these things? Dinah was just visiting her neighbours. As we noted when looking at Hagar's story, it is all too easy for survivors

---

3   See Amanda Duberman, '34 Things Women Do To Stay Safe Show The Burden of "Being Careful"', 7 May 1015 and updated 7 December 2017, www.huffingtonpost.co.uk/entry/what-women-have-to-do-to-be-careful_n_7072080 [Accessed November 2020 and October 2022]

GOD THE RESCUER (DINAH)

of rape to blame themselves. We must condemn the rapists themselves, and not leave any room for women to assume guilt for their own abuse.

Dinah's brothers came in from their work in the fields as soon as they heard that Dinah had been raped. Simeon and Levi are significant characters in the story; the ones who take action to avenge Shechem's crime. The rest of Dinah's brothers then loot the city and take all the women and children. I can't help wondering whether this means they raped them and forced them into marriage. Did Dinah's rape lead to more rape as well as murder?

We will talk a lot about the male characters in Dinah's story and the other stories in this study. There are two important reasons for this:

1. Some of the stories don't give us much information about the female characters at all, which, as we will see here, actually tells us a lot.
2. Gender-based violence is not a feminist issue, it is a global issue. It affects us all, whether we know it or not.

The male characters in these stories have much to teach us about how God views violence committed by men against women and girls. We are all part of the story.

Notes

VIOLENCE AGAINST WOMEN

 **Discussion Starters**

1. Throughout the passage we never once hear from Dinah herself. Her voice is silent. Do you think this is significant?

2. Genesis 34:3 tells us that Shechem loved Dinah. Do you think this is true?

3. Why do you think Jacob kept quiet about Dinah's rape when he first heard about it?

4. What kind of message did Jacob's inaction give his daughter Dinah?

GOD THE RESCUER (DINAH)

5. In this story, how does Shechem's father Hamor stand in stark contrast to Jacob, as a parent?

6. Are Simeon and Levi the heroes in this story? Discuss their possible motives for killing the men of Shechem.

7. Dinah's brothers tell Hamor and Shechem that the men of their city must be circumcised if they want to intermarry with the Israelites. This is a misrepresentation of the covenant sign of circumcision. Why is this sinful?

8. Jacob condemns Simeon and Levi on his deathbed in Genesis 49:5–7. The consequences of this curse reveal each man's motives in the eyes of God. Simeon's tribe became the smallest in Israel and was eventually swallowed up within the much larger tribe of Judah. The Levites became the priests of the nation of Israel. So, should we conclude that Levi is the hero in this story?

Personal Application

Dinah was raped. Her 'no', whether it was expressed out loud or simply the absence of a 'yes', didn't matter to Shechem. I wonder which lies of the enemy Dinah believed as a result of the rape. Did she believe her voice didn't matter? That she didn't matter? That God didn't care about her? And did the actions of her family reinforce those lies? Dinah is never mentioned again in the Bible, apart from her name in a genealogical list in Genesis 46:15. Perhaps this is why – the enemy took her out of the race. Spend some time in prayer asking God whether He wants to correct any lies you've believed.

Seeing Jesus in the Scriptures

Shechem's actions were sinful, against Dinah and against the people of God. Dinah's traumatic story tells us that rape is abhorrent to God and we are supposed to be outraged by it. We are supposed to grasp how precious Dinah is to God – so precious that it is an absolute tragedy that no one protected her, by rescuing her from Shechem's house and giving her a choice between marrying Shechem or allowing his execution.

Dinah mattered to God. Dinah was created in the image of God and was chosen and appointed by God to be a fruitful member of His family. The actions of the other characters in Dinah's story only reinforced the enemy's lies. Dinah needed a saviour. Dinah needed someone to rescue her and none of her family members acted the way they should have done, leaving us feeling hopeless about Dinah's future. The people of God were in desperate need of the Saviour, the Rescuer, someone who would give a voice to the oppressed, bring freedom to the captives, spread peace and not violence. The story points to our need for Jesus. We cannot be rescued by other imperfect people, even our family members, any more than by our own actions. Salvation comes through Him alone.

WEEK THREE
God the Father (Jephthah's Daughter)

Opening Exercise

Do you have any funny or sweet stories of your own children, or children you know, running to answer the door when the doorbell rings?

Bible Readings

- Judges 11
- Leviticus 18:21
- 2 Kings 23:10

Optional Readings
- Deuteronomy 12:31
- Deuteronomy 18:10
- Exodus 15:19–21
- 1 Samuel 18:6–7
- Leviticus 27

VIOLENCE AGAINST WOMEN

 Opening Our Eyes

The mighty warrior Jephthah, faced with his Ammonite enemies, made a vow to God – that if God would give the Ammonites into his hands in battle, then Jephthah would sacrifice whatever came out to meet him on his return home. Jephthah defeated the Ammonites and acted on his vow by sacrificing his daughter, his only child.

You may be wondering whether this story really belongs here. If Jephthah had a son rather than a daughter it could have been a male child sacrificed, couldn't it? Is this really an example of gender-based violence? Well, it wasn't a male child. This is a historical account of a father murdering his daughter. I can't help wondering whether the story would have ended differently if Jephthah had a son. The stark reality is that thousands of female children all over the world are killed every year, through selective abortion and infanticide. Young female lives are seen as less valuable than their male counterparts in some cultures and are thrown away without hindrance. If Jephthah's child had been a son rather than a daughter, would he have placed more value on the child's life? Would he have trusted God to intervene like Abraham did in Genesis 22:8, or would he have wished to die in place of his child like David did in 2 Samuel 18:33? Perhaps Jephthah was lacking in faith and character compared to those leaders.

We must read this story in the context of the book of Judges as whole. Judges 2:10 tells us that 'another generation grew up who neither knew the LORD nor what he had done for Israel'. But Jephthah supposedly knew God and the history of Israel; the elders went to him because they knew there was something different about him. Jephthah knew God better than anyone else in his generation.

We are supposed to be shocked by Jephthah's story and ponder how this man of great faith and godly character, one

GOD THE FATHER (JEPHTHAH'S DAUGHTER)

of the 'good guys', could possibly descend to such a low as to murder his only child. It all starts with a promise, a vow Jephthah foolishly makes to God almost immediately after being filled with the Holy Spirit. Why did Jephthah make this vow, and did he actually know the likely consequences of it?

Jephthah may have known God better than anyone else in his generation, but unfortunately as the story unfolds we see that there were gaps in Jephthah's knowledge and understanding, of both Scripture and God's character.

Notes

VIOLENCE AGAINST WOMEN

Discussion Starters

1. Why do you think the elders of Jephthah's clan asked him to return to the fold to be their leader when the Ammonites started a war against Israel?

2. What evidence is there in the story that Jephthah knew the Scriptures?

3. Jephthah's vow to the Lord is set out in Judges 11:30–31. In light of Leviticus 18:21 and 2 Kings 23:10, do you have any ideas as to why Jephthah made this vow?

4. What do you think Jephthah's vow reveals about his faith for victory in the battle?

GOD THE FATHER (JEPHTHAH'S DAUGHTER)

5. Who or what do you think Jephthah expected to greet him when he returned home from battle? Are there any reasons why he should have known it would be his daughter?

6. Can you pinpoint the reasons why Jephthah's daughter's death is so tragic?

7. Why do you think Jephthah's daughter urged her father to carry out his vow?

8. Jephthah should never have made his vow to God in the first place, but what do you think he should have done when his daughter greeted him and he realised what it meant?

Personal Application

If Jephthah, the leading man of God in his generation, could lose sight of fundamental truths in his walk with God because of his failure to study God's Word, then it stands to reason that so can we. Jephthah forgot who God is; that He is merciful, kind, loving and forgiving. He also forgot that every person is made in God's image and each life is a precious gift.

How often do you read the Bible? Has a poor understanding or selective reading of Scripture ever led you to make a mistake that you later became aware of? This could be a good time to look at your daily routine and when you spend time with God. God calls us into a personal relationship with Him – we can only really know someone when we spend quality time with them. If you don't currently spend time with God regularly, reading the Bible and praying, consider whether you need to prioritise time with God over something else?

Seeing Jesus in the Scriptures

The story of Jephthah's daughter is about a leader, a rescuer, who falls short; with disastrous consequences for someone he loves and for the people of God as a whole. The story points to the need for the Saviour, the Rescuer – Jesus, the perfect leader. The One who doesn't just know the Word of God, but who is the Word of God. Jesus was fully human, yet fully God. Salvation would not come through any human leader, family member, judge or king (as we'll see in next week's study), but only through God Himself.

Our God specialises in resurrection life. In the story of God's people, death does not get the final word. Not Jephthah's daughter's death, and not Jesus' death. In Him, all stories will be resolved. Everything will be turned around for good. He redeems all things. In Him, there is hope.

WEEK FOUR
God the Loving Husband (The Unnamed Concubine)

Opening Exercise

Think about a couple whose marriage inspires you, and then discuss as a group what inspiring marriages look like, giving practical examples.

Bible Readings

- Judges 19

Optional Readings
- Judges 20
- Judges 21
- Genesis 19:4–8

Opening Our Eyes

Judges 19 tells the horrific story of a woman who is neglected, sacrificed, gang-raped, murdered and dismembered; brutalised and then annihilated. Her voice is silent and her name isn't even recorded. This is arguably the most violent and disturbing story in the whole canon of Scripture, bar the story of the crucifixion when humanity murdered the living God.

The woman in this story is described as a 'concubine'. The Hebrew word used here is *pileghesh* and there is some debate over her status – was she a slave, a wife or something in between? And does it matter? A concubine was traditionally a secondary wife used to produce more offspring, or for sexual pleasure. In some cultures it is also used to mean a lower-status wife who has not received a bride price. It is interesting that there is no mention of a primary wife in the story. The word *pileghesh* seems to be used to denote ownership and give us a sense of the woman's low social status.

In this study we will take a close look at the woman's relationship with the Levite, the man in the story described at times as 'her husband' and later in the story as 'her master'. Judges 19:2 tells us that the woman was unfaithful to her husband the Levite and left him, but there is also debate over what this means; some translations suggest sexual infidelity, but some suggest that the very act of leaving him is what made her 'unfaithful'. Some translations even say she left because she was angry with him. *The Message* translation says 'she quarrelled with him and left'. It is very possible that the Levite was already abusive and his treatment of her is what caused her to leave. I prefer this explanation because the picture of an abusive relationship is borne out in the rest of the story and the Levite's later behaviour would seem irrational and out of place if not in the context of an already abusive relationship. In addition, the woman returned to her family home; she didn't leave her husband to be with a new lover. This seems to fit more with the idea that she had

GOD THE LOVING HUSBAND (THE UNNAMED CONCUBINE)

been treated badly and sought comfort and protection from her parents. If the woman had committed adultery it's unlikely she would have travelled to her family home, where she would have brought shame on her family and where she could have been easily found and brought to justice.

This woman's story is one of being owned, of being possessed by others. Just as in the story of Dinah in Genesis 34, this unnamed woman's voice is entirely absent, her thoughts and wishes irrelevant.

Notes

VIOLENCE AGAINST WOMEN

Discussion Starters

1. Apart from the shocking act at the very centre of the story, when the Levite gives the woman over to be gang-raped by the men of Gibeah, can you find any other evidence in the passage that this is an abusive relationship?

2. Why do you think the woman's father was so keen to entertain the Levite and spend more time with him? Was it for her benefit?

3. Why do you think the wicked men of Gibeah pounded on the door and demanded to take the Levite and rape him?

4. Who killed the Levite's concubine?

GOD THE LOVING HUSBAND (THE UNNAMED CONCUBINE)

5. Does anything strike you about the Levite's explanation of what happened in Judges 20:4–7?

6. The remaining tribes of Israel proclaim in Judges 19:30 that 'such a thing has never been seen or done', is that true?

7. The Israelites' solution to this tragedy, which began with a violent gang rape and murder, appears to be more rape and murder. Have you ever considered the link between war and sexual violence? Pause here to reflect on the consequences of war on women and children. Identify one current war zone and pray for the women and children caught up in the conflict.

8. Can you identify the clues within the final chapters of Judges which tell us that the Israelites were acting well outside the will of God?

Personal Application

The Levite's relationship with his concubine was one of abuse; he displayed entitlement and ownership over her, as well as a total lack of empathy for her. Have you ever thought about these characteristics of an abusive relationship before? We can all feel entitled and lack empathy at times. Spend some time in prayer asking God whether there is something in your character, or in one of your relationships, He wants to change.

It was not God's will for the twelve tribes of His family to turn against one another in war; they were supposed to live in peace with God and with one another. The story shows that when God's people no longer live in relationship with Him, their relationships with one another soon breakdown too, with terrible consequences. How important is your relationship with God to your closest relationships?

Seeing Jesus in the Scriptures

The shocking act of sexual violence in this story is there to tell us loud and clear that the perpetrators are acting outside the will of God. As we begin to understand the purpose of the story, we understand that God finds their crime even more abhorrent than we do. We are supposed to see this story as an absolute tragedy. The Israelites desperately needed a saviour and no human judge could save them. They tried to exercise justice themselves and become their own saviours, which only led to grave sin and further tragedy. The story points to Jesus, because no one else could save them from their sin. In contrast to the Levite in the story, God is described in the Bible as being like a loving husband. The Church is described as His bride. God does not exercise entitlement and ownership over us, or lack empathy for us. Through Jesus we, the Church, are reconciled to our loving husband. The God who is merciful and compassionate, slow to anger and abounding in love.

WEEK 5
God the King of Kings (Tamar)

Opening Exercise

Can you think of anyone who is a powerful advocate for others? Discuss whether you find it easier to stand up for yourself or to stand up and speak out for the rights of others.

Bible Reading

- 2 Samuel 13

Optional Readings
- Psalm 51

Opening Our Eyes

In 2 Samuel 13 we read the story of Tamar, a princess, the daughter of King David, who is raped by her half-brother Amnon. It is only when we consider Tamar's story as part of the wider story of David's family that we begin to understand what it teaches us about sexual assault, and about sin in general.

Tamar was probably in her late teens when Amnon raped her. David married the mother of Absalom and Tamar after he became king of Judah in 1010BC. In accordance with the culture of ancient Israel, Tamar's role as an unmarried teenager was to take care of the men in her family. In this story we see that her kindness and commitment to that role left her vulnerable to exploitation. She gladly went to Amnon's house, on the instructions of her father David, to take care of him. There is no indication that Tamar suspected anything untoward, she acted in good faith and obedience, with no reason not to go. All over the world, women and girls are lured into danger every day by people close to them. Sexual violence is most likely to be inflicted by a family member or intimate partner, not a stranger. If there were no such story of sexual violence within a family in the Bible, we might be indignant that women's experience of suffering wasn't accurately portrayed by Scripture. Tamar's story reassures us that God understands the full breadth of human suffering.

Tamar stands out in this study as one of the few female characters given a voice in her story. We hear Tamar's refusal loud and clear and should be struck by her presence of mind in a situation of serious danger. The fight, flight or freeze response is part of the body's natural response to protect us from danger. It is common for women to freeze, or completely dissociate, in response to the threat of sexual violence. To freeze physically, but also to become incapable of speech, as if the body is shutting down. Men can find it difficult to understand this instinctive survival response, as their response to danger

GOD THE KING OF KINGS (TAMAR)

might more typically be fight or flight. At times this has led to questions around whether a female victim of sexual violence was actually consenting. I am always in awe of women I read about who managed to fight off their attackers. Tamar not only found her voice and stood her ground, but also came up with various cunning ways to try and talk Amnon out of raping her. Tamar has a voice in the story, but unfortunately no one listens and Amnon overpowers her.

Notes

VIOLENCE AGAINST WOMEN

 **Discussion Starters**

1. Is this a love story? Was Amnon in love with Tamar? Or was she in love with him?

2. How did Tamar attempt to stop Amnon from raping her?

3. Why do you think Tamar raised the idea of marriage?

4. What were the immediate and long-term consequences of the rape for Tamar?

GOD THE KING OF KINGS (TAMAR)

5. Why did Amnon's feelings for Tamar quickly turn to intense hatred (2 Samuel 13:15)?

6. How was Amnon's cousin Jonadab an accessory to the rape of Tamar?

7. Why do you think Absalom told Tamar to keep quiet about the rape? If Absalom was trying to be a loving brother to Tamar and help her, how did he miss the mark?

8. Why do you think King David didn't bring Amnon to justice?

Personal Application

One of the troubling things about David's reaction to the rape of Tamar is that there is no communication recorded between David and his daughter. Not only did David fail to give Tamar justice, but he didn't even comfort her in her distress or do anything to mitigate her desolation. Later in the story David and all his servants are seen to mourn and weep bitterly day after day, not for Tamar, but for the perpetrator Amnon and for Absalom. In David's neglect of Tamar we might even read that he regarded Tamar as property, just like Amnon did. If someone you know was assaulted, how might you comfort them and help them seek justice? Is there someone God has already called you to support and advocate for?

Seeing Jesus in the Scriptures

We are supposed to see Tamar's rape by Amnon as one of the terrible consequences of David's sin in taking Bathsheba as his wife and having Uriah killed. We are supposed to get the absolute tragedy of it, for Tamar herself and for the entire family and royal line of David. In contrast to the story of the unnamed concubine in Judges, in Tamar's story there is a king in Israel – but here even royalty still does what is right in its own eyes. David failed to do justice in Israel, or even within his own family. No human king could ever save Israel from its sin. Tamar's story points to the need for a different kind of King; it points to Jesus.

Identifying David, 'a man after [God's] own heart' (Acts 13:22), as a terrible father and king might leave us feeling hopeless. David was no stranger to failure, but he did have his heart set on following and obeying God, and he repented of his sin. Psalm 51 is David's prayer of repentance, after taking Bathsheba. David knew God could forgive him and change him. David had hope and so can we. Our hope is in Jesus.

WEEK SIX
God the Just Judge (The Woman Caught in Adultery)

Opening Exercise

There are many stories of Jesus conversing with women in the Gospels – which is your favourite, or the one that first springs to mind, and why?

Bible Reading

- John 8:1–11
- John 7:37–38

Optional Readings
- Isaiah 55:1–3
- Leviticus 20:10
- John 18:31

 **Opening Our Eyes**

All the stories we have looked at so far point to the need for Jesus, so let's now take a look at how Jesus treated women. The woman caught in adultery described in John 8 would have certainly become a victim of gender-based violence, if not for Jesus' intervention. Her story foretells the death of Jesus on the cross as an act of costly sacrificial love and it shows us that Jesus is the answer to the injustices of abuse now.

You may notice that at the beginning of chapter 8 of John's Gospel there is a note explaining that this story wasn't included in the earliest manuscripts. There are three possible reasons for this:

1. The story is a work of fiction.
2. It was passed down only through word of mouth, in the oral tradition, and it was eventually included in the written account.
3. It was left out when families paid for a copy to be made by hand, because they didn't want their daughters committing adultery and saying they should be forgiven because of Jesus' example. Other Christians were brave enough to include the story in their copies, despite its potential to offend within the Jewish culture.[4]

Many scholars are convinced that the woman's story is a historical account. It is interesting to note that cultural attitudes to women may even have impacted its inclusion in Scripture.

This story stands out as different in the context of this book, because this woman was guilty of sexual sin. The other women we've looked at so far were wholly innocent in relation to their specific stories, with the exception of the unnamed concubine

---

[4] I owe this thought, and a great deal of this study, to Kenneth E Bailey, *Jesus Through Middle Eastern Eyes: Cultural Studies in the Gospels* (London: SPCK, 2008)

GOD THE JUST JUDGE (THE WOMAN CAUGHT IN ADULTERY)

who may or may not have been unfaithful to her husband. If we are looking for Jesus' heart for women, then far better to look at the story of a guilty, sinful woman. If you want to know someone's heart, whether they are compassionate and loving, it is important to look at how they treat the guilty, the sinner, the one that others treat with contempt.

This woman doesn't stand out as different when we take a broader look at Jesus' interactions with women. Consider Jesus' reaction to the sinful woman who poured perfume on His feet at Simon the Pharisee's house (Luke 7:36–50) and his friendship with Mary Magdalene (Luke 8:1–3), the first person to see Him after His resurrection (Mark 16:9, John 20:10–18). Jesus was filled with compassion for women who had been cast out of society as a result of their own sin and their treatment by others. He made time for them, he forgave their sins, healed them and welcomed them in. Are we, the Church, following His lead?

Notes

Discussion Starters

1. This story actually starts in the previous chapter when Jesus took a passage about God from Isaiah 55:1–3 and applied it to Himself. How did this challenge the religious teachers?

2. Picture yourself in the woman's shoes for a moment. What do you imagine she was wearing? What do you imagine she was thinking, feeling and anticipating?

3. What do you think happened to the man that the woman was committing adultery with? That particular sin does take two people!

4. How did the religious teachers entrap Jesus?

GOD THE JUST JUDGE (THE WOMAN CAUGHT IN ADULTERY)

5. What was the significance of the fact it was the day after a major feast day (John 7:37)?

6. Why did Jesus write on the ground with His finger? Have you heard any helpful teaching on this point?

7. Why do you think Jesus invited anyone without sin to throw the first stone at the woman in John 8:7?

8. How did Jesus save the woman's life and what was the cost?

Personal Application

If you are a woman who has suffered gender-based violence, no matter what you have done or what has been done to you, God invites you into relationship with Himself through the cross of Jesus. Just as God sought Hagar out in the wilderness, invited her to know Him and made promises to her, He extends that invitation to you. Jesus laid down His life for you. He knows you and He loves you. He has plans for your future.

If you are a man who has perpetrated abuse or violence against women, no matter what you have done or what has been done to you, God invites you into relationship with Himself through the cross of Jesus. In this story Jesus reminded the crowd of men and the woman that they had all sinned and needed to change. If you repent of your sin, you will be forgiven. God loves you and wants to transform you into the likeness of His Son.

Even if you haven't been directly affected by male violence against women, I invite you to see the beauty of God's salvation plan revealed in the stories we've explored.

Seeing Jesus in the Scriptures

In this story we discover Jesus as El Roi, the God who sees our suffering and is moved to act out of love and compassion. Jesus is the answer to the problem of male violence against women. He laid down His life to bring forgiveness, redemption, restoration, and transformation by the power of the Holy Spirit.

In saving the woman's life, Jesus foretold the story of the cross. He paid the penalty for our sin with His own life, that we may be reconciled to God. This is how Jesus responds to violence against women. This story demonstrates the life-changing power of the costly love of God.

WEEK SEVEN
What Needs to Change?

Opening Exercise

If you could speak to one of the characters from one of the stories we have studied (not including Jesus), which person would you choose and what would you most like to tell them?

Bible Reading

- Exodus 34:6
- Matthew 22:36–40
- Romans 3:22–24
- Romans 5:8
- 2 Corinthians 3:18
- Galatians 5:22–25
- Philippians 2:3–7

Optional Readings
- Genesis 1:26–27
- Genesis 3:16
- Matthew 28:19
- Ephesians 5:8–11

 ## Opening Our Eyes

Before we turn our thoughts to the future and what needs to change to end all forms of violence against women and girls, let's first remember that every person on earth is created by God and bears His image. This gives us a baseline of equality – every life equal in value, worthy of dignity and respect. Genesis 3 tells us that gender inequality and male violence against women is a consequence of the Fall, of sin entering and corrupting the world. This is not how God intended it to be. It was supposed to be a beautiful and perfect partnership.

Jesus' life, death and resurrection was and is God's perfect plan to restore us to relationship with Himself, but also to restore the earth to His original design, to restore our relationships with one another. One day we will have eternal life and there will be no more violence or injustice. But it's not just about what happens when we die, is it? Jesus is God's plan for now. He is the answer to the injustices we experience on earth today.

We know that a huge shift in attitudes and culture is required if we want to see an end to violence against women. It can be easy to feel hopeless in the face of such a challenge. But there is hope and His name is Jesus. The power of the Holy Spirit – the same power that raised Jesus from death, the power to transform – now lives in us, His Church. We are each being transformed into His likeness as the Holy Spirit bears fruit within us. We are part of the answer to injustice, oppression and violence. God has chosen to use us to change the world, to spread this transformative power across the globe.

Let's start by changing the attitudes and culture within the Church. By loving one another and those around us. By living so differently from the world around us that it can't go unnoticed. Imagine what would happen if the Church eradicated domestic abuse from within its 'walls'. If there were no more stories in the news of sexual abuse committed by church leaders abusing

WHAT NEEDS TO CHANGE?

their positions of authority. That would be powerful, wouldn't it? That really would demonstrate the love of God and His mighty power.

I pray that God will bless you richly and make you more like Jesus and that you would know the transformative power of the gospel in your life, particularly in relation to your relationships and interactions with the opposite sex.

Notes

Discussion Starters

1. Can you identify any themes or attitudes common to the biblical stories of violence against women we have looked at in this study?

2. Can you recall any recent local, national or international news stories of violence against women? Were any of those themes or attitudes a factor?

3. How might the attitudes and culture within the Church make a difference in the fight to end violence against women and girls?

4. How does our salvation in Jesus challenge our sense of entitlement?

WHAT NEEDS TO CHANGE?

5. How does our sanctification (God transforming us into the likeness of Jesus) and discipleship challenge our sense of entitlement and our prejudices (including misogyny)?

6. Why is being part of a church family important for our sanctification?

7. What could you do within your church or small group setting to encourage and increase empathy and understanding between the sexes?

8. What could your church do, and what could you do personally, to make your church a safer place for women to tell their stories of abuse and seek help and healing?

Personal Application

As the people of God, charged with sharing the gospel and discipling others, we are all on the frontline in the fight for justice. We must challenge entitlement and encourage empathy within the Church if we want to see the kingdom of God affect the culture around us and bring an end to violence against women and girls. We are all called to play a part. Spend some time in prayer asking God what He's called you to do. You may also want to pray for your church and for more of the Holy Spirit.

Seeing Jesus in the Scriptures

Exodus 34:6 tells us that God is compassionate and gracious, slow to anger, abounding in love and faithfulness. In Week 1 we saw the character of God at work in the story of Hagar, a survivor of sexual violence who was seen and heard by the Lord. In Weeks 2 to 5 we saw that no human leader could bring true justice, an end to violence and oppression. In Week 6 we saw Jesus, the character of God incarnate (Phil. 2:3–7), demonstrating His compassion and abundant love by rescuing the woman caught in adultery and redirecting the anger and hatred of the Pharisees and teachers of the law towards Himself.

Jesus laid down His life for all, that anyone who puts their trust in Him might be saved and transformed. Whatever your history, God wants to rescue you and transform you into the likeness of His Son (2 Cor. 3:18), through the work of the Holy Spirit (Gal. 5:22–25).

The kingdom of God changes everything – for individuals, for relationships, for churches and for whole communities. What would your church be like if every member thought and behaved like Jesus? What would your town or city look like if every Christian was thinking and behaving that way? That would surely have an impact! Let's start with us.

Leader's Notes

These Leader's Notes have been written to support you as you lead your small group. They will help you interpret these stories of abuse and unpick what we can learn from them and their inclusion in Scripture. Male violence against women and girls is a heavy subject and the conversation may be difficult at times. It may be more difficult for some members of the group than others. Please tell the group in advance that you are planning to look at what the Bible says about violence against women. Encourage discussion but close down any argument. If it becomes clear that someone in your group is struggling with the topic, you may want to speak to them in private to offer a listening ear or point them to more appropriate support.

WEEK ONE: The God Who Sees Me

Opening Exercise
The aim is to get the group thinking about how we use the various names and attributes of God to increase our faith in prayer for specific things, or when we have seen God move. For example, when I am sick I will declare that God is 'Jehovah Rapha', the Lord who heals.

Discussion Starters

1. Get the group talking about consent and whether this is a story of rape. There are four factors you may want to consider:

  a. Hagar wasn't consulted at all. She wasn't given a voice or a choice in this part of the story.
  b. Abraham and Sarah talked about Hagar as if they owned her and were entitled to use her body to produce a child. Experts suggest it's this attitude of ownership and entitlement that underpins all relationships of domestic abuse.
  c. There was a mismatch of power and authority here. Abraham was 86 and Hagar was probably much younger. Abraham was the head of the community and Hagar was a servant.
  d. This isn't really a story of marriage. The word 'wife' isn't used again in relation to Hagar and in later chapters she's referred to as Sarah's servant. The word is used here to show that Sarah gave Hagar into a sexual relationship with Abraham. There was no ongoing relationship, she was just used as a surrogate.

2. Abraham and Sarah had been waiting eleven years for God to fulfil His promise to them and they were beginning to lose hope. They both sinned by taking matters into their own hands, deciding that if God was not going to give them a child, then they would find a way to make it happen for themselves. Their plan also amounted to serious sexual sin. Abraham was previously a man of great faith, walking in radical obedience to God.

3. You may want to encourage the group to consider Abraham's monogamy up to this point, Sarah's years of infertility and her time in Egypt in Genesis 12:10–20, plus the risks to Hagar and her unborn baby in the desert. Be sensitive to any infertility issues or marriage difficulties within the group.

LEADER'S NOTES

4. The 'angel of the Lord' was either an angel messenger speaking the words of God on His behalf, or it was God the Son, the preincarnate Christ. I like to picture Jesus meeting with Hagar in the desert, because it helps me to remember the character of God. In the past this story has been used to tell abused women to return to their abusive marriages, but this is an erroneous interpretation. Hagar was at risk in the desert, but that's not the only reason God sent her back. Encourage the group to look ahead to God's covenant with Abraham in Genesis 17. God invited Hagar into relationship with Him in the desert and made promises to her, then Hagar and Ishmael were included in the covenant as part of God's family.

5. In Job 39:5–8 God used the image of a wild donkey to talk about freedom. God was telling Hagar to return to servitude, but promised that He had a plan for her, and that her son would be free. Perhaps it's no surprise that Hagar took comfort from this.

6. Encourage discussion around the consequences of sexual abuse for the victim. Hagar clearly felt unseen, unheard, insignificant. She wasn't given a voice or a choice to consent to sex with Abraham or not. This would have led to a false belief that her voice didn't matter; that she didn't matter – God speaking to her would have challenged this beautifully.

7. Ishmael was born as a result of Abraham and Sarah's sin and the violation of their marriage covenant. God could not allow that violation to be the means through which He would fulfil His promise. On top of that, right from the story of Cain and Abel in Genesis 4 we see that God wants us to rely on Him and not on the work of our own hands. Abraham sinned by taking matters into his own hands. God had to do it all, so that the glory would go to Him.

8. Genesis 21 reveals that Abraham never treated Hagar as his wife, but it also shows that Abraham loved Ishmael. Abraham was distressed at the thought of having to send him away and knew it would be evil. In contrast to his lack of faith in Genesis 16, Abraham sought the Lord in Genesis 21 and obeyed God's command to send Hagar and Ishmael away. Abraham had to live with the consequences of his sin. He surrendered his beloved son into God's hands. This was an act of faith.

WEEK TWO: God the Rescuer

Opening Exercise
The aim is to get the group thinking about what a hero or rescuer looks like and how we might approach the Scriptures with an expectation that some characters are 'goodies' and some are 'baddies'.

Discussion Starters
1. Dinah's silence is significant because it:

   a. Reinforces the idea of Dinah's powerlessness.
   b. Reminds us that Dinah had been kidnapped by Shechem and was away from her family, where the focus of the story is.
   c. Tells us that Dinah isn't the main character. The point or lesson of the chapter lies elsewhere; it's not really about the crime or its effects on Dinah. But that doesn't mean the passage tells us nothing about how God views sexual assault.

Dinah wasn't even consulted when the male characters discussed the subject of her marriage. Although the book of Deuteronomy was probably written well after the events of Genesis 34, Hamor's request to Jacob, to give Dinah in marriage to Shechem, indicates that the law set out in Deuteronomy 22:28–29 was already well established. Verse 29 commands the perpetrator to marry, but not the victim. Marriage was the rape victim's legal right if she decided it was preferable to

LEADER'S NOTES

remaining unmarried (unsuitable for marriage to another) and a financial burden on her parents. Dinah should have been given a voice to respond to that request. She was supposed to have a choice. It is significant that no one in the story gave Dinah that choice. No one seemed to think her voice mattered.

2. The language of Genesis 34:2 leaves no room for discussion over whether the sex was consensual. Not only does the language indicate violence, but there's no indication that Shechem and Dinah had met before or had built up any kind of relationship. This is a story of one incident, not a relationship over time. This all makes verse three problematic. Rape is not an act of love; it is an abuse of power and an act of violence. And when we consider the lack of a pre-existing relationship we see that Shechem can't possibly have loved Dinah when he raped her. Perhaps verse three is included to show us that Shechem himself thought he was in love. A modern-day understanding of sexual violence and abuse would identify Shechem's beliefs of ownership and entitlement (reflected in his language) as the root cause of the abuse in this story. These beliefs underpin all relationships of domestic abuse.

3. You may want to encourage the group to look back at Genesis 32 and 33 to get an idea of Jacob's character. There are several verses in these preceding chapters and several clues in the story that speak of Jacob's fear:

   a. Genesis 32:7 says that with great 'fear and distress' Jacob prepared to meet his brother Esau.
   b. In Genesis 32:11 Jacob prayed, 'Save me, I pray, from the hand of my brother Esau, for I am afraid he will come and attack me, and also the mothers with their children.'
   c. In Genesis 33:16–20 we read that, after his tearful reunion with Esau, Jacob declined to build his home in Seir where Esau lived and instead set up camp in Canaan. Jacob was afraid that Esau would change

his mind about forgiving him for stealing their father Isaac's blessing. This left Jacob and his family vulnerable to the Canaanites – like Shechem.

   d. In Genesis 34:30, after the rape of Dinah, Jacob said to Simeon and Levi, 'You have brought trouble on me by making me obnoxious to... the people living in this land. We are few in number, and if they join forces against me and attack me, I and my household will be destroyed.' Jacob was afraid of the Canaanites – even with the protection of his sons.

4. Jacob did nothing while Dinah was held captive in Shechem's house following a violent attack. This is hardly the behaviour of a loving father. Perhaps Jacob's inaction gave Dinah the message that she didn't matter, adding to her trauma.

5. While Jacob failed to protect his daughter and his family's honour, Hamor didn't hesitate to stand up for his son, despite knowing he'd committed a terrible crime. Hamor and Jacob were both terrible fathers, but in very different ways. It is possible that Dinah's kidnap and rape were planned by Hamor and his son to secure the marriage and an ongoing relationship of trade with wealthy Jacob and his family. Dinah's rape made her unmarriageable in that culture. Hamor and Shechem knew that her only option for marriage would be to marry Shechem.

6. There are three possible motives that drove Simeon and Levi to kill the men of Shechem:

   a. Protecting Dinah's honour and rescuing her from further harm.
   b. Protecting the honour, integrity and purity of the family of God.
   c. Selfishly protecting their own honour and taking revenge for Shechem's affront to it.

LEADER'S NOTES

You may want to have a quick look at Genesis 46:10 when discussing motive b). Simeon married a Canaanite woman and had a son by her, so Simeon clearly wasn't as concerned with the purity of God's people as it first appears.

7. In Genesis 17:11 God told Abraham that as a sign of the covenant between them every male of eight days old, born into his household or bought with money, must be circumcised. By telling the men of the city of Shechem to be circumcised, Dinah's brothers cheapened the sacred sign of circumcision, making it available to anyone, and used it as a vehicle for deception and violence. There are three reasons why this was sinful:

   a. God hates deceit, it is Satan who is 'the father of lies' (John 8:44).
   b. Circumcision was a gift from God, a special sign of His covenant with His people, which they abused.
   c. They used this deceit to weaken their enemy so that they could attack the city, instead of trusting God to give them the victory.

8. The problem was that Levi failed to honour his sister Dinah and give her a voice, he deceived Shechem and Hamor, he misused the gift of circumcision, the special sign of God's covenant with His people, and he took matters into his own hands instead of trusting God. Not only that, but his actions led to yet more violence. Levi is the closest we get to a hero in this story, and yet he still fell very short.

WEEK THREE: God the Father

Opening Exercise
The aim is to get the group to see how obvious it would have been to Jephthah that his daughter would be the first to greet

him on his return home, as well as to start thinking about the tragedy of the story.

Discussion Starters

1. Judges 11:1 expressly tells us that Jephthah was a mighty warrior; that's the kind of military leader you need in a war. But there are also some clues as to a less obvious reason why they went to Jephthah. The name Jephthah means 'he opens'. Although it's a fact of history, Jephthah's name is like a literary clue to help us understand the story. The elders chose Jephthah to lead them because he read the Scriptures.

2. Encourage the group to look for evidence in the passage. Examples include the following:

   a. In Judges 11:9 Jephthah reminded the elders of Gilead that the Lord alone could grant them victory over the Ammonites.
   b. In Judges 11:15–22 Jephthah corrected the Ammonite king's false account of Israel's history – a history he would have known from reading, or being well taught in, the Scriptures.
   c. In Judges 11:27 Jephthah stated that the Lord is the true Judge or ruler of Israel. He refused to take the title that rightly belongs to God.
   d. Not only did Jephthah read the Scriptures, but they also clearly had an impact on him. His reading and his relationship with God impacted his character. Rather than being bitter that his brothers drove him away, Jephthah was forgiving and willing to fight for the family of God. He also took the elders to the tabernacle at Mizpah to seek the will of God before taking action against the Ammonites. God even filled Jephthah with the Holy Spirit; an honour not open to all God's people at that time.

3. Jephthah may well have known God, seemingly better than anyone else in his generation, but either that still didn't amount to knowing God very well, or he forgot who his God was. The main god of the Ammonites was a god called Molech. To worship Molech, people sacrificed their sons and daughters. Jephthah seemed to imagine His God to be similar to the gods of those around him – the gods who demanded child sacrifice.[5] Jephthah lost sight of what it means to be part of the family of God, different from the people around him, including his enemies the Ammonites.

4. Jephthah's vow was an act of unfaithfulness. He pressed God for help that was already his through the Holy Spirit. Jephthah desired to bind God. Having been filled with the Holy Spirit, Jephthah lost sight of who the Holy Spirit is. He lacked faith in the power of God dwelling within him to win the battle. He forgot that by filling him with the Holy Spirit, God had already marked him out as the victor.

5. Some children are always first to the door when someone knocks, no matter how many times they are told not to open the door for strangers or deliveries. Even more obedient, sensible or cautious children are often enthusiastic about answering the door when they know it's a parent returning from a trip, particularly if they might be bearing gifts or important news. Perhaps Jephthah thought a servant or a niece or nephew might greet him, rather than his own daughter, but he must have known that his child could be first to the door. Not only that, but Jephthah's daughter's greeting with dancing and tambourines was traditional in ancient Israel. In Exodus 15:19–21 Miriam and all the women sang and danced with tambourines after the defeat of the Egyptians at the Red Sea, and (centuries later) in 1 Samuel 18:6–7 the women greeted King Saul with singing and dancing, with tambourines and lutes, when David had killed Goliath the Philistine.

---

5   I owe this thought, and a great deal of this study, to Phil Moore and his talk on Jephthah at the New Ground conference, Ashburnham 2013.

6. Deuteronomy 12:31 and Deuteronomy 18:10 tell us specifically that the murder of Jephthah's daughter was a sin. Death is always a tragedy because, although it is a sure part of life, it goes against God's original design for humankind. Jephthah's daughter's death is especially tragic because it was premature, violent, sinful and it cut off the family tree – Jephthah's daughter was an only child with no children herself. We are supposed to understand that Jephthah forfeited the next generation of worshippers because he didn't understand the Word of God. Jephthah was called to lead the nation of Israel, but failed to even lead his family and raise up the next generation of believers.

7. Unfortunately, Jephthah's daughter didn't know the Scriptures well either. Jephthah had clearly raised his daughter to be compassionate and obedient, but he had failed to teach her to know God through His Word.

8. Encourage the group to discuss repentance. You may also want to discuss Leviticus 27, which allowed for a substitution to be made, in the form of a redemptive payment, when a person's life was dedicated to God. In 1 Samuel 1:11 Hannah made a vow to give her unborn child (Samuel) to God, but the expectation was that he would serve in the Temple, not that he would be destroyed! Each person was assigned a value, according to their age and 'usefulness', so they could be set free from their obligation by the payment of money. Jephthah could have made an alternative offering to God. (Leviticus 27:29 is about the destruction of God's enemies, for example in 1 Samuel 15 where King Saul was commanded to bring God's judgment against the Amalekites, not about people devoted or given in a vow to God.)

LEADER'S NOTES

WEEK 4: God the Loving Husband

Opening Exercise
The aim is to start thinking about what good relationships look like, in order to be able to recognise an unhealthy or abusive relationship.

Discussion Starters
1. Evidence that this relationship is abusive may include the following:

   a. In some translations (including the NIVUK) Judges 19:3 only tells us that 'her husband went to her to persuade her to return', but some other translations add that he went to 'speak to her heart', 'speak kindly' (ESV, KJV) to her, 'speak personally' (NLT) to her, or 'win her back' (*The Message*). As far as we know, this tender conversation never actually took place.
   b. The Levite waited four months before travelling to Bethlehem to ask her to return – hardly a sign of true love and commitment!
   c. It's not as if we are always left guessing when we read about relationships. The Bible writers do often tell us, or clearly indicate how people felt about their spouses, by their words and their actions. If the Levite loved this woman, it is likely the writer of Judges would have told us explicitly.
   d. If people within your group are reading from different Bible translations, you may notice that in some version of Judges 19:19 the Levite called the woman 'your maidservant' (RSV), 'your handmaid' (AMP, KJV) or 'your female servant' (ESV, NET) when he was speaking to the old man in the town square in Gibeah. He referred to his own concubine as the old man's property, offering her up to gain his favour. The Levite demonstrated the attitude of ownership and entitlement that underpins the cycle of abuse.

2. The tribe of Levi were the priests of the people of God, entrusted to protect and uphold the holiness of God's set-apart people. Perhaps the Levite was an influential man and the father thought his hospitality would benefit him in the future. There is nothing at all to indicate that the woman's father was pressing the Levite to stay for her benefit. If the woman left her husband at the beginning of the story due to abusive behaviour, then the woman's father joined the ranks as yet another man who abused her by failing to protect her and handing her over to the Levite. Her father wasn't at all concerned when the Levite neglected the woman by spending time eating and drinking with him, thereby leaving her out, because he was complicit in that neglect.

3. The men's demand for access to the Levite wasn't about sexual desire. It was about power and humiliation. They clearly didn't want outsiders in their community, as their first sin was their failure to offer the Levite hospitality when he arrived in town. No one from the tribe of Benjamin offered to host him and then they attempted to run the Levite out of town using sexual violence. This parallels the events of Sodom and Gomorrah in Genesis 19:4–8.

4. It is possible that the woman died in the doorway of the house or on the journey home, as a result of the brutal gang rape. The Amplified Bible says in Judges 19:28, 'But there was no answer [for she had died]', but that line is missing from most modern translations, leaving some ambiguity and allowing the interpretation that she was still alive when the Levite picked up his knife.

5. All the Israelites assembled to hear what happened and the Levite changed the story to leave out the fact the men of Gibeah wanted to rape him, and that he gave the woman up in his place, to protect himself and his reputation. The Levite called the rest of the tribes of Israel to action against the men of Gibeah and the tribe of Benjamin, by sending his wife's body

parts to them, resulting in the first civil war between the family of God. The Levite was clearly driven by a need for personal revenge, not by righteous anger at the rape of his wife.

6. Unfortunately, although the story is indeed shocking, we are supposed to see this as hyperbole; the statement is just not true. Time and again the people of God departed from His will and despicable abuse and violence resulted. We see from the rest of the story, in Judges 20 and 21, that the Israelites weren't as shocked by the crime as they made out. It didn't stop them dead in their tracks and cause them to repent. They united against the ones they saw as sinful, without pausing to examine their own hearts before God. Although, the Israelites did seek God with regard to their fight against the Benjamites, having almost destroyed the whole tribe of Benjamin as a result, they then reverted to doing what was right in their own eyes.

7. In this story, 400 young women from Jabesh Gilead and 200 girls from Shiloh were kidnapped and forced into marriage to rebuild the tribe of Benjamin. On top of that, having already murdered all the women and children of the tribe of Benjamin, and all but 600 of the men, the Israelites put to death the rest of the people of Jabesh Gilead (Judg. 21:10–11).

8. The statement 'In those days Israel had no king; everyone did as they saw fit' appears in Judges 17:6 and Judges 21:25, and is partly repeated in Judges 18:1 and Judges 19:1. We are supposed to understand that the Israelites had strayed far from the will of God. These men of Gibeah in particular were refusing to submit to God's Word and were doing whatever they wanted to do, which was evil in God's sight. The shocking act of sexual violence tells us loud and clear that the perpetrators were acting outside the will of God.

WEEK FIVE: God the King of Kings

Opening Exercise
This should get the group thinking about how difficult it is to speak out in the face of oppression or abuse. It may also highlight a difference between the sexes in this regard. This will help you appreciate how extraordinary Tamar was in standing up to the man who intended to rape and ruin her.

Discussion Starters
1. The beginning of the story is told from Amnon's point of view. 2 Samuel 13:2 shows that Amnon wanted to sleep with Tamar; he didn't want to marry her. This is a story of lust, not love. Amnon viewed Tamar as an object of lust from the beginning and his focus was on doing things to her. He plotted to get her alone entirely for his own interests. I am reminded of Dinah's story in Genesis 34, which states that Shechem loved her and spoke tenderly to her... after he'd kidnapped and raped her. This too is a story of deceit and rape; abuse, not love. I reject the idea that Tamar was in love with Amnon and desired to be his wife. Following the rape, Tamar refused to leave Amnon's house and implored him not to send her away, but not because she loved him – rather because she understood the dreadful, lasting consequences of the rape for her.

2. We hear Tamar's refusal loud and clear in 2 Samuel 13:12. She called Amnon 'brother' in response to him calling her 'sister', but also to remind him of their relationship as siblings, in the hope that would stop him in his tracks. When that didn't work, she made three further attempts, appealing to Amnon's compassion, his pride and his reason, setting out the consequences for Amnon and pleading with him to think carefully and change his mind.

3. Tamar raised the idea of marriage to try and stop Amnon from taking her by force. She offered an alternative solution to his lust. There is some controversy over the interpretation of incest laws and whether they were in effect at the time of David. If they were, then perhaps Tamar was stalling for time, clutching at straws even though she knew their marriage was prohibited. Maybe Tamar hoped Amnon would go to her father and be rebuked, putting an end to the matter. Perhaps Tamar actually thought her father may allow the marriage. There was some precedent for allowing such a union; Sarah and Abraham had the same father but different mothers (Genesis 20:12). Given David's own sexual impropriety and his bending of the laws, it is reasonable to conclude that he may have permitted the marriage.

4. Tamar knew that if Amnon would not marry her then she must live out her days as an outcast, single and childless, unsuitable for marriage to another. We read that Tamar lived in Absalom's house, 'a desolate woman' (v.20). The word for 'desolate' here is a word used to refer to a land that is laid waste. In terms of long-term consequences, I wonder what Amnon's refusal to respect Tamar's 'no' taught her. Did she believe the lies of the enemy as a result? Did she believe that her voice didn't matter? We are not told when Tamar died, but within seven years of the rape Absalom named his own daughter Tamar (2 Samuel 14:27). In some traditions such naming is only done in memory of a deceased relative. Perhaps through Amnon's sin the enemy took Tamar out of the story.

5. There are three possible reasons for Amnon's hatred that you may want to discuss:

   a. Amnon raped Tamar because he wanted to have her sexually, but also because he wanted to hurt her for saying 'no' to him; such was the magnitude of his sense of entitlement. Following the rape, Amnon blamed Tamar, because she turned him down. In his view, if Tamar had consented to sleep with him then he would not have had to take her by force.

b. Lying before him in disarray and suffering, Tamar reminded Amnon of his sin and his weakness. He was repulsed by her because of what he had done to her.
   c. If Tamar's perfect virginity or purity was one of the things that made her attractive to Amnon, then he had turned her into 'damaged goods' and taken away that beauty. We read that Amnon said to his servant 'Get this woman out of my sight and bolt the door after her' (v.17). In the original Hebrew Amnon didn't call her 'this woman', only 'this'. Tamar had become an object, used and discarded.

6. Jonadab called Amnon 'the king's son' (v.4), reminding him of his entitlement as heir to the throne. An attitude of entitlement is often the root cause of rape, especially in a situation of domestic violence like this one. Not only that, but Jonadab also came up with the plan for Amnon to get Tamar alone, therefore Jonadab must share in Amnon's guilt.

7. We know that Absalom was angry at what Amnon had done and hated him for it, so either Absalom wanted to keep the whole thing quiet to protect the royal family's reputation, or Absalom was saying 'be quiet for now' (i.e. for the time being) so that he could plan revenge against Amnon. Unfortunately, even if Absalom was trying to be a loving brother to Tamar and help her, he missed the mark in the following ways:

   a. Absalom took the power to act out of Tamar's hands and further disempowered her by assuming a right to avenge her as he saw fit. There is no evidence that he consulted her in his plan to kill Amnon.
   b. In telling Tamar to be quiet, Absalom also reinforced the lie that Tamar's voice didn't matter. Not only that, but we have no idea whether Tamar understood Absalom's hint that he planned to seek revenge, so it's possible Tamar thought he was silencing her and ignoring Amnon's sin entirely.

LEADER'S NOTES

    c. Absalom told Tamar to stifle her feelings when he said, 'Don't take this thing to heart (v.20)'. She was not encouraged to express her feelings. Absalom didn't even tell Tamar he was angry, or comfort her in any way.

8. There are several possible reasons for David's inaction:

    a. Perhaps David could not live with the hypocrisy of bringing Amnon to justice when he had escaped justice for sexual sin and murder himself.
    b. Perhaps David felt that he shared in Amnon's guilt because he delivered Tamar into Amnon's hands.
    c. Perhaps David's love for Amnon prevented him from sentencing him to death.
    d. Perhaps it was fear that stopped David from doing justice, because Amnon was heir to the throne and if he and his men had fought back they could have killed David and taken the kingdom.

WEEK SIX: God the Just Judge

Opening Exercise
This exercise is designed to get the group talking about the character of God, revealed in Jesus in the context of His interactions with women.

Discussion Starters
1. Jesus challenged the scribes and the Pharisees (the religious teachers) with regard to the application of the Law by applying it to Himself. Jesus was the promised Messiah, God incarnate, so he was perfectly right to apply those words to himself. But His declaration challenged the religious teachers to choose; was He the Messiah, or just a man guilty of blasphemy? If they did not believe He was the Messiah, then according to the Law they needed to order His arrest. It forced their hand. The crowd

was confused and divided. Some accused Jesus of blasphemy, while others wondered if perhaps He was the promised Messiah, or a prophet. The scribes and the Pharisees wanted to arrest Jesus, but they couldn't because of His popularity. His arrest would have caused uproar.

2. This woman had been caught in bed with a man who was not her husband. Was she naked? Dressed hastily in the dark, perhaps in bed linen? She may have felt shame – for her sin, her nakedness, or both. She would have known the penalty for the crime of adultery, so she must have been terrified, anticipating a violent, painful death. The fact that we don't even know this woman's name reflects her powerlessness in the situation. She wasn't given an opportunity to explain what happened, or repent of her sin.

3. The Mosaic Law stated that both parties to adultery should be stoned to death (Lev. 20:10). Discuss the fact that they caught her in the act, but not the man involved. Perhaps her lover was one of them. Perhaps the whole thing was a set-up and she was lured into sin while he was allowed to disappear. Maybe they allowed him to escape purely because he was a man like them, or for some other reason. They didn't require both parties in order to trap Jesus.

4. Rather than challenging Jesus with a hypothetical question, the scribes and the Pharisees pushed the woman in front of Jesus, quoted the Law of Moses and then they challenged Him directly. Under Roman rule the Jews did not have the right to execute anyone (John 18:31), so the way the scribes and the Pharisees saw it, Jesus had two options:

    a. To go with a strict application of the Law of Moses and state that the woman should be put to death by stoning.

LEADER'S NOTES

    b. To explain that He couldn't obey the Law of Moses strictly because of the current political situation, so allowances had to be made.

Option a) would have certainly led to Jesus' immediate arrest by the Romans. Civil unrest often began in the Temple, so the Romans had easy access to the Temple from their military fort. Option b) would have seen Jesus accused of being a coward and discredited as a rabbi. The trap they set for Him was planned to ensure He lost either way.

5. The day after any major feast was observed as a Sabbath, so no work was allowed.

6. Jesus couldn't have verbally decreed the death penalty in front of the Roman guards without being arrested immediately (and leaving the woman to the crowd). He also couldn't write His answer down on a scroll, because the rabbis defined writing as work. Writing with a finger in the dust was allowed because it left no permanent mark. These rules were written down centuries after the events in John 8, but this account of Jesus tells us that they were in force then. By writing in the dust Jesus demonstrated that He was not only familiar with the written Law but also with the developing oral tradition of that Law. He showed that He was educated and observed the rules strictly. By what happens next, we can conclude that Jesus must have written something like 'stone her'.

7. You might be surprised by Jesus' invitation, if you know His reputation for compassion and His heart for sinners. But Jesus didn't actually want them to execute her, it was all part of His plan to save her. Jesus knew that when a crowd stoned someone to death no one bore responsibility for it; they were all just part of the mob. Jesus asked every individual to acknowledge responsibility for their participation in the act. He presented the crowd with a dilemma. By ordering the woman's execution he showed that he was willing to go to jail for the Law of Moses. But were they? The Roman guards would certainly ask who threw the first stone and arrest them. But that's not all. The crowd knew that according to Scripture no one is without sin (see, for example, Isa. 53:6 and Ecc. 7:20), so if someone stepped out claiming to be sinless, they would be shouted down and put to shame.

8. The woman was expecting a violent and painful death, but by the end of the story Jesus had shifted the attention and anger from her to Himself. She was free to walk away. This demonstration of unexpected love saved the woman's life. Discuss how the story foretells Jesus' sacrifice on the cross.

WEEK SEVEN: What Needs to Change?

Opening Exercise
This final study is an opportunity to think back on all the stories we have looked at. Identifying an important message for one of the biblical characters should help you think about the messages the Church could be giving survivors and perpetrators of abuse.

Discussion Starters
1. Common themes include: the male characters' sense of entitlement and ownership over the female characters; a lack of empathy; a poor understanding of the value of human lives made in the image of God; the silencing of female voices and dire (at times fatal) consequences for the female characters.

2. Unfortunately, it is unlikely you will have any trouble calling to mind a recent news story. You may recall a story of murder, rape, assault, domestic abuse, kidnap, sexual exploitation, child marriage or rape as a weapon of war. Consider the elements of entitlement and lack of empathy, in particular.

LEADER'S NOTES

3. If the gospel of Jesus Christ changes hearts, minds and lives, then it can also change marriages, change whole churches and transform entire towns and cities. If a shift in attitudes and culture is required, let's change the attitudes and culture within the Church and lead the way. Discourage any use of 'us and them' language – we know, from the statistics and from abuses that have come to light, there are both victims and perpetrators of abuse within the Church.

4. When someone is convicted of their sin and saved (justified) by the grace of God, that must by definition erode any sense of entitlement. We become aware of our own sin and separation from God, that we are not worthy to be in relationship with Him and don't deserve anything. Yet Jesus saves us anyway. It's not about us; it's all about Him. Jesus challenges our sense of entitlement by His humility; He was actually entitled to equality with God and yet He gave His life for each one of us.

5. Discuss the fruits of the Holy Spirit (love, joy, peace, patience, kindness, goodness, faithfulness, gentleness and self-control). As they grow within us, they are in direct conflict with self-serving entitlement. As we are sanctified, we should grow in humility and seek to put the needs of others first, as Jesus did. Therefore, the way that we are discipled and the way that we disciple other Christians is fundamental in the fight against gender-based violence.

6. Discuss Jesus' commandment to 'love your neighbour' in Matthew 22:39. As we interact with one another, as part of a church family, we all grow in our understanding of others, in our empathy and in our love for one another. It is significant that the first thing God says about His character when He talks to Moses in Exodus 34 is that He is compassionate. God is sanctifying us, making us more like Him, and His heart is moved by the suffering of others. Compassion is closely related to empathy; first you understand the feelings of others and then you are moved by them.

7. One way we can help this process of increasing empathy is by encouraging people to tell their own stories and share their thoughts and feelings, making space in our church meetings for testimonies. We can also make sure that when we discuss or teach on Bible stories with various characters, including female characters, we try to enter into the story and think about how each character felt and the consequences for each person. That might be difficult at times. In this area of violence against women, another thing we can and must do is raise up more female preachers. The Church needs to hear more female voices on a Sunday morning, especially but not just on this issue of injustice.

8. Any response will be personal, but ideas could include the following:

Suggestions for individuals:

a. Regularly read the biblical stories of violence against women and pray for an end to such violence.
b. Raise any male entitlement and lack of empathy with your church leaders when those issues arise.
c. Encourage female leaders and preachers.
d. Encourage empathy within the church by sharing your own testimonies.
e. If a victim of abuse tells you their story, listen to them, believe them and follow the church's procedures to support them.
f. Consider attending training on the issue from an outside organisation.
g. Give generously to charities tackling violence and abuse, both at home and abroad.

LEADER'S NOTES

Suggestions for churches:

a. Teach on a Bible story relating to gender-based violence regularly, with the same regularity that you teach on sexuality or racial diversity.
b. Challenge any male entitlement and lack of empathy directly when those issues arise.
c. Discourage male entitlement by thinking about diversity, raising up female leaders and hearing from female preachers.
d. Avoid having any meeting with only male leaders at the front.
e. Encourage empathy within the church by making room for testimonies and hearing from various teachers, rather than relying on one or two preachers.
f. Make the church a safe place for victims of abuse to report, by listening, believing and having robust procedures in place to protect them.
g. Contact an outside organisation (for example Restored) for training and support on the issue (see the Signposting section at the back of the book for details).
h. Give generously to charities tackling violence and abuse, both at home and abroad.
i. Pray for the work of organisations and systems tackling violence against women, including the criminal justice system and the government (local and national).
j. Consider speaking into the wider culture in your local area by responding to relevant consultations and attending relevant forums and think tanks.

Daily Guide

This Daily Guide is designed to help you to engage with the material in the Study Guide between the sessions. More copies of this daily guide are available to download for free from **wvly.org/c2ccv**.

Day 1 Read through Week One in the Study Guide.

Day 2 Pray for someone you know who is pregnant, or someone who is suffering from, or has suffered from, fertility issues.

Day 3 Do something kind for a single parent in your community. You may want to pray for them or offer some practical help, kind words or a gift.

Day 4 Pray for the work of a local, national or international charity that supports survivors of modern slavery.

Day 5 Find out what your name means and ask God whether it reflects the truth about you, or whether He calls you by another name.

Day 6 Meditate on Isaiah 41:10. Can you think of anyone in the Bible, other than Hagar, who received comfort from God with the words 'Do not be afraid' (Hagar received them in Gen. 21:17)?

Day 7 Can you recall a promise God has made to you, either personally in prayer, or in the Bible? Thank God for His promises to you.

Day 8 Read through Week Two in the Study Guide.

Day 9	Reflect on a recent news story of kidnapping or rape and pray for all the people involved, including the victim(s) and the perpetrator(s). Pray for justice if there is an ongoing investigation or court case.
Day 10	Meditate on Psalm 139:1–18 and reflect on how precious you are, and how precious Dinah was, to God.
Day 11	Remind someone in your life how much you value them and how precious they are to God. You may want to use words or a small gift, or you may want to do something kind for them.
Day 12	Think about which character in Dinah's story you most identify with and why.
Day 13	Pray for the justice system, including the police, the courts and the prison service.
Day 14	It is important not to get weighed down by the tragedy of injustice. Spend time in prayer acknowledging that justice is God's mission and responsibility, He simply invites us to get involved. Give any anxiety or sadness you are feeling as a result of this study to God.
Day 15	Read through Week Three in the Study Guide.
Day 16	Pray for someone you know who has lost a child.
Day 17	Meditate on Psalm 78:1–7 and reflect on your own role in teaching the next generation of worshippers.
Day 18	Meditate on Exodus 34:4–7 and remind yourself who God is.
Day 19	Ask God whether you have ever made an unhelpful inner vow.
Day 20	Think about when and how often you read the Bible. Could there be a better time in your day to do it? Could you read it more often or for longer periods? Ask God what He wants you to commit to.
Day 21	Pray for more fruit of the Holy Spirit in your life. Pray, in particular, for increased joy.
Day 22	Read through Week Four in the Study Guide.
Day 23	Pray for someone you know who is in an abusive or unhappy marriage, or has been in one in the past.

DAILY GUIDE

Day 24 Do something kind for someone who is divorced, separated or widowed. You may want to pray for them or offer some practical help, kind words or a gift.

Day 25 Meditate on Genesis 6:6,13. Reflect on how much God hates the violence of humankind.

Day 26 Pray for the work of a local or national charity that supports survivors of domestic abuse.

Day 27 Pray for a country or region currently at war. Pray for an end to the conflict. Pray, in particular, for the women and children and pray against rape as a weapon of war.

Day 28 Pray for more fruit of the Holy Spirit in your life. Pray, in particular, for increased peace.

Day 29 Read through Week Five in the Study Guide.

Day 30 Pray for the work of a local or national charity that supports survivors of sexual assault and rape.

Day 31 Martin Luther portrayed Tamar and Amnon as a couple in love and ignored the violence of Tamar's story altogether. John Calvin focused on Tamar as the greater sinner and concluded that the harm done to her by Amnon came from God as a just punishment. Reflect on how those interpretations enforce harmful attitudes within the Church.

Day 32 Do something kind for one of your siblings, if you have any, or someone you know who is an only child. You may want to pray for them or offer some practical help, kind words or a gift.

Day 33 Would you know how to respond to someone who confided in you following sexual violence or abuse? Consider asking your church and/or your employer if there is a policy or guidance you should be familiar with.

Day 34 Reflect on whether there are any significant events in your own family history that have had serious consequences down through the generations.

Day 35 Pray for the royal family and/or the government in your own nation, for salvation and wisdom.

Day 36 Read through Week Six in the Study Guide.

Day 37 Reflect on a recent news story of an 'honour-based' killing and pray for all the people involved, including the perpetrator(s). Pray for justice if there is an ongoing investigation or court case.

Day 38 Meditate on Isaiah 43:1–2 and reflect on how precious you are to God.

Day 39 Reflect on how Jesus has changed your life by his costly sacrifice on the cross.

Day 40 Meditate on Micah 6:8 and reflect on your own role in bringing about justice in your community and the wider world.

Day 41 Ask God specifically what He wants you to do to make your church a safer place for women in general and for survivors of gender-based violence in particular.

Day 42 Pray for more fruit of the Holy Spirit in your life. Pray, in particular, for increased kindness.

Day 43 Read through Week Seven in the Study Guide.

Signposting

Crisis Support

Find support locally: Women's Aid
Women's Aid is a grassroots federation working together to provide life-saving services in England and build a future where domestic abuse is not tolerated. Their directory contains up-to-date information about domestic abuse support services across the UK, so you can find the right local support when you need it most.

www.womensaid.org.uk

Refuge
Refuge supports women, children and men experiencing domestic violence with a range of services, including the National Domestic Abuse helpline.

www.refuge.org.uk

The National Domestic Abuse Helpline
This is a free, confidential, 24-hour helpline.

0808 2000 247

You can also use their live chat online service Monday to Friday, from 3pm to 10pm.

www.nationaldahelpline.org.uk

Mental Health Support

Counselling
The NHS defines counselling as a 'talking therapy that involves a trained therapist listening to you and helping you find ways to deal with emotional issues'.

The Counselling Directory website includes a nationwide database of qualified counsellors and therapists, an advanced search tool and a section explaining the different forms of therapy used by practitioners and how they can help.

www.counselling-directory.org.uk

Waverley Abbey Trust
Waverley Abbey College provides training in the areas of counselling, leadership, spiritual formation and chaplaincy. Their teaching is practical, based on theory and rooted within a biblical framework. Their Find a Counsellor Directory will help you find a Christian Waverley Abbey College trained counsellor in your local area.

www.waverleyabbeycollege.ac.uk/find-a-counsellor

EMDR therapists
EMDR stands for Eye Movement Desensitisation and Reprocessing. It is a unique, powerful therapy that helps people recover from problems triggered by traumatic events in their lives. It stops difficult memories causing so much distress by helping the brain to reprocess them properly. EMDR is best known for treating post-traumatic stress disorder (PTSD) and it can also help with a range of mental health conditions in people of all ages.

Rape Crisis
Rape Crisis England & Wales have just launched a new 24/7 Rape and Sexual Abuse Support Line.

SIGNPOSTING

0808 500 2222 247

sexualabusesupport.org.uk

Relevant Charities

Press Red
Press Red is a Christian organisation educating, equipping and empowering on the issues of violence and abuse against women and girls. They make people aware of the injustices happening worldwide and on our doorstep, providing them with the tools and resources they need to make a difference.

www.pressred.org

Restored
Restored believe that the Church is the hope of the world and should be taking the lead in challenging injustice wherever it is found. They want to see a network of churches that never tolerate abuse, but instead provide a safe refuge for survivors. They work to equip the Church to end domestic abuse and bring dignity and fresh hope to survivors.

www.restored-uk.org

International Justice Mission
IJM is the largest anti-slavery and human trafficking organisation in the world. IJM is a global team of lawyers, social workers, community activists and other professionals working to protect people in poverty from violence. Their teams combat slavery, trafficking and violence against women and children, and other forms of abuse. They are fighting for a world where all are free.

www.ijmuk.org

The Cover to Cover Bible Study Series

CHARACTERS

Abraham
Adventures of faith
ISBN: 978-1-78259-089-7

Barnabas
Son of encouragement
ISBN: 978-1-85345-911-5

David
A man after God's own heart
ISBN: 978-1-78259-444-4

Elijah
A man and his God
ISBN: 978-1-85345-575-9

Elisha
A lesson in faithfulness
ISBN: 978-1-78259-494-9

Jacob
Taking hold of God's blessing
ISBN: 978-1-78259-685-1

Joseph
The power of forgiveness and reconciliation
ISBN: 978-1-85345-252-9

Mary
The mother of Jesus
ISBN: 978-1-78259-402-8

Moses
Face to face with God
ISBN: 978-1-85345-336-6

THEMES

Bible Genres
Hearing what the
Bible really says
ISBN: 978-1-85345-987-0

Covenants
God's promises and
their relevance today
ISBN: 978-1-85345-255-0

The Creed
Belief in action
ISBN: 978-1-78259-202-0

The Divine Blueprint
God's extraordinary
power in ordinary lives
ISBN: 978-1-85345-292-5

Fruit of the Spirit
Growing more like Jesus
ISBN: 978-1-85345-375-5

God's Rescue Plan
Finding God's fingerprints
on human history
ISBN: 978-1-85345-294-9

Great Prayers of the Bible
Applying them to
our lives today
ISBN: 978-1-85345-253-6

The Holy Spirit
Understanding and
experiencing Him
ISBN: 978-1-85345-254-3

The Image of God
His attributes and character
ISBN: 978-1-85345-228-4

Names of God
Exploring the depths
of God's character
ISBN: 978-1-85345-680-0

NEW: Revival
Seeking and encountering
abundant life
ISBN: 978-1-78951-441-4

Rivers of Justice
Responding to God's call
to righteousness today
ISBN: 978-1-85345-339-7

The Second Coming
Living in the light of
Jesus' return
ISBN: 978-1-85345-422-6

The Uniqueness of our Faith
What makes Christianity
distinctive?
ISBN: 978-1-85345-232-1

NEW: Violence against Women
Discovering El Roi,
The God Who Sees
ISBN: 978-1-78951-445-2

NEW TESTAMENT

NEW: Matthew
Your Kingdom Come
ISBN: 978-1-78951-450-6

Mark
Life as it is meant to be lived
ISBN: 978-1-85345-233-8

Luke
A prescription for living
ISBN: 978-1-78259-270-9

John's Gospel
Exploring the seven miraculous
signs
ISBN: 978-1-85345-295-6

Acts 1–12
Church on the move
ISBN: 978-1-85345-574-2

Acts 13–28
To the ends of the earth
ISBN: 978-1-85345-592-6

The Letter to the Romans
Good news for everyone
ISBN: 978-1-85345-250-5

1 Corinthians
Growing a Spirit-filled church
ISBN: 978-1-85345-374-8

2 Corinthians
Restoring harmony
ISBN: 978-1-85345-551-3

Galatians
Freedom in Christ
ISBN: 978-1-85345-648-0

Ephesians
Claiming your inheritance
ISBN: 978-1-85345-229-1

Philippians
Living for the sake
of the gospel
ISBN: 978-1-85345-421-9

The Letter to the Colossians
In Christ alone
ISBN: 978-1-855345-405-9

Thessalonians
Building Church in
changing times
ISBN: 978-1-78259-443-7

1 Timothy
Healthy churches –
effective Christians
ISBN: 978-1-85345-291-8

2 Timothy and Titus
Vital Christianity
ISBN: 978-1-85345-338-0

Philemon
From slavery to freedom
ISBN: 978-1-85345-453-0

Hebrews
Jesus – simply the best
ISBN: 978-1-85345-337-3

James
Faith in action
ISBN: 978-1-85345-293-2

1 Peter
Good reasons for hope
ISBN: 978-1-78259-088-0

2 Peter
Living in the light of
God's promises
ISBN: 978-1-78259-403-1

1,2,3 John
Walking in the truth
ISBN: 978-1-78259-763-6

Revelation 1–3
Christ's call to the Church
ISBN: 978-1-85345-461-5

Revelation 4–22
The Lamb wins! Christ's
final victory
ISBN: 978-1-85345-411-0

The Armour of God
Living in His strength
ISBN: 978-1-78259-583-0

The Beatitudes
Immersed in the grace of Christ
ISBN: 978-1-78259-495-6

The Lord's Prayer
Praying Jesus' way
ISBN: 978-1-85345-460-8

Parables
Communicating God on earth
ISBN: 978-1-85345-340-3

Prayers of Jesus
Hearing His heartbeat
ISBN: 978-1-85345-647-3

The Prodigal Son
Amazing grace
ISBN: 978-1-85345-412-7

The Sermon on the Mount
Life within the new covenant
ISBN: 978-1-85345-370-0

OLD TESTAMENT

Genesis 1–11
Foundations of reality
ISBN: 978-1-85345-404-2

Genesis 12–50
Founding fathers of faith
ISBN: 978-1-78259-960-9

Exodus
God's Epic Rescue
ISBN: 978-1-78951-272-4

The Ten Commandments
Living God's Way
ISBN: 978-1-85345-593-5

Joshua 1–10
Hand in hand with God
ISBN: 978-1-85345-542-7

Joshua 11–24
Called to service
ISBN: 978-1-78951-138-3

Judges 1–8
The spiral of faith
ISBN: 978-1-85345-681-7

Judges 9–21
Learning to live God's way
ISBN: 978-1-85345-910-8

Ruth
Loving kindness in action
ISBN: 978-1-85345-231-5

Nehemiah
Principles for life
ISBN: 978-1-85345-335-9

Esther
For such a time as this
ISBN: 978-1-85345-511-7

Job
The source of wisdom
ISBN: 978-1-78259-992-0

Psalms
Songs of life
ISBN: 978-1-78951-240-3

23rd Psalm
The Lord is my shepherd
ISBN: 978-1-85345-449-3

Proverbs
Living a life of wisdom
ISBN: 978-1-85345-373-1

Ecclesiastes
Hard questions and
spiritual answers
ISBN: 978-1-85345-371-7

Song of Songs
A celebration of love
ISBN: 978-1-78259-959-3

Isaiah 1–39
Prophet to the nations
ISBN: 978-1-85345-510-0

Isaiah 40–66
Prophet of restoration
ISBN: 978-1-85345-550-6

Jeremiah
The passionate prophet
ISBN: 978-1-85345-372-4

Ezekiel
A prophet for all times
ISBN: 978-1-78259-836-7

Daniel
Living boldly for God
ISBN: 978-1-85345-986-3

Hosea
The love that never fails
ISBN: 978-1-85345-290-1

Joel
Getting real with God
ISBN: 978-1-78951-927-2

Jonah
Rescued from the depths
ISBN: 978-1-78259-762-9

Habakkuk
Choosing God's way
ISBN: 978-1-78259-843-5

Haggai
Motivating God's people
ISBN: 978-1-78259-686-8

Zechariah
Seeing God's bigger picture
ISBN: 978-1-78951-263-2

For current prices or to order, visit waverleyabbeytrust.org/publishing